THE

Woodworker's

MANUAL OF FINISHING AND POLISHING

by Charles D. Cliffe

Argus Books Limited
1 Golden Square
London W1R 3AB
England

© Argus Books Ltd., 1986

ISBN 0 85242 882 0

Printed by The Bemrose Press/Cheshire Typesetters Ltd.,
Hunter House, 8 Canal Street, Chester.

Contents

Introduction

FROM its earliest issues *Woodworker* magazine has, through 'Question Box', answered readers' questions on all aspects of woodworking. A subject which has frequently appeared is that of wood finishing. This is due to a number of reasons. Having spent a great deal of time and care on construction, the woodworker wishes to enhance his work by skilfully applying the appropriate finish. The completed job must harmonise with the rest of the furniture in the house; it must not be glaringly amateurish. It must never proclaim itself 'home made'.

For some years I have endeavoured through written articles, demonstrations and practical tuition to explain the various stages which must be gone through to achieve a 'professional' finish. Quite often my pupils have remarked: 'That sort of information never appears in books'. Because of this, and also the fact that an amazingly large number of people of all ages and walks of life have shown such interest in wood finishing, I decided to describe the various processes in the clearest possible manner.

Careful preparation of the surfaces to be polished is essential. Any skimping of one stage of the work is sure to be revealed and indeed magnified later on. Perfection at all times is the aim and must be achieved if the final result is to be entirely satisfactory. It is for this reason that sharpening and using the steel cabinet scraper has been described in some detail. This simple tool gives trouble not only to beginners but also to many experienced tradesmen. When properly sharpened it is ideal for taking out the marks left by the smoothing plane or removing the finest of shavings from a piece of cross-grained hardwood.

Glasspapering, which follows scraping, presents few difficulties but staining can be rather more troublesome and is in consequence described more fully. The important thing to remember is to experiment on pieces of waste wood from the job in hand to make sure that the colour is right. Then and only then, should the stain be applied to the finished piece.

Polishers generally have a wide range of ready mixed stains in their workshops and it is sometimes remarked that we are a secretive breed because most of our preparations are unlabelled. There are two reasons for the absence of labels. Firstly, there is no need because we know the contents of all our bottles and jars and, secondly, any labels there might be would soon be made illegible through being handled by fingers discoloured with stain and polish. For try as we might we cannot keep our hands completely free from the marks of our trade. For the less experienced it is sound advice to label everything clearly. It is very easy to confuse raw linseed oil with transparent white french polish, their appearance is so similar.

Cleanliness should be observed at all times, a greasy thumbprint or a flake of dried shellac from a finger nail can wreck what might otherwise have been perfection.

There are many, particularly amongst the retired and those about to retire, who wish to repair and restore antiques. This can be most interesting and rewarding work and immense satisfaction can be gained from putting an attractive piece into good working and decorative condition. Before repolishing previously french polished work, do master the technique of polishing new wood first. Not only are there different approaches between old and new work but polishing experience is necessary to judge whether the original finish can be rubbed down or must be completely removed.

Knowledge of the different varieties of polish is needed to judge which polish will produce the desired finish.

Mistakes will inevitably occur, but we learn from our experiences and with practice comes improvement so if you are considering trying your hand at polishing, roll up your sleeves and get started.

I am sure that you will find the work most absorbing and I wish you every success.

Charles Cliffe

ONE The workshop and its equipment

FREQUENTLY instructions regarding the making of pieces of furniture end in one brief sentence and the whole art of wood finishing is dismissed: 'After thoroughly glasspapering the piece was then stained to the desired colour and given two coats of polyurethane varnish.'

Before we consider the numerous finishes available, let us take a look at our workshop and see what it should be like. For a start we shall need plenty of light, preferably daylight, so that we can see exactly what we are doing and that any stains we use are the colour we want. Mixing stains in artificial light is a tricky business and sometimes gives disappointing results. Dust is a great enemy of the polisher and regular use of a vacuum cleaner will help to prevent dust from settling on and spoiling polished surfaces which are still soft. Temperature is also important and should be maintained between 65°F and 70°F. If the temperature is too low, french polish and varnish will chill and become cloudy. Similarly work which has been in a cold atmosphere should not be polished until it has been allowed to stand in warm surroundings for several hours. Damp and draughts must also be eliminated if we are to turn out good work.

The bench should be near a window and the polisher should stand behind it so that the work is between him and the light. This will give maximum visibility and enable all stages of polishing to be carried out correctly.

As in all things, careful preparation is essential. A coat of paint may disguise and diminish minor defects, but with polishing the reverse is the case. Minor

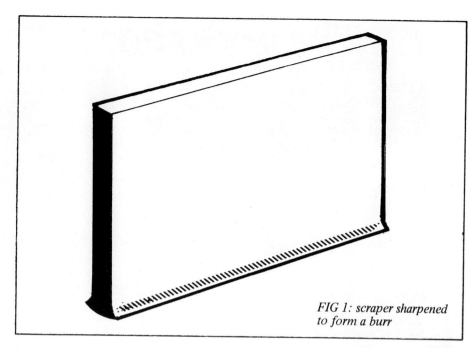

FIG 1: scraper sharpened to form a burr

defects are magnified and highlighted once polish is applied so perfection is our aim.

Even a well set smoothing plane can leave visible plane marks behind it, particularly on curly grained woods. Removal of the marks with a steel cabinet scraper is the next stage. This is a flat rectangular piece of steel about 4in long, 3in wide and up to 1/8in thick. They are obtainable from most tool shops, although many tradesmen make their own from a piece of saw blade. The long edges are sharpened to form a burr (Fig 1) the cutting action of which removes very fine shavings without tearing even cross-grained woods. It is an ideal tool for cleaning up veneers, inlay and cross-banding.

PHOTO ONE: filing the edges square

5

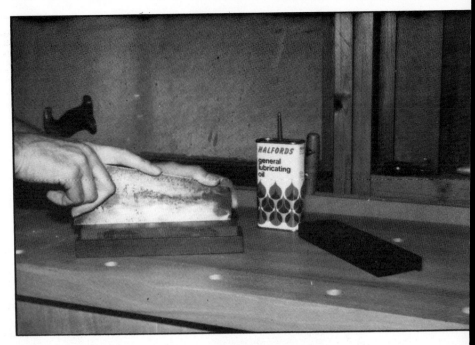

Although a simple tool, it needs a practised hand to sharpen it so that it cuts properly. Firstly it must be gripped in the vice and the edge filed straight and square (photo 1). To remove these file marks, the edge of the scraper is now rubbed on the oilstone (photo 2). To prevent the stone from being worn hollow the edge of the stone is often used for this operation. The scraper is then placed flat on the stone (photo 3) and rubbed along the stone to remove any burr which may have formed. It is wiped clean of oil and placed flat on the bench and with the back of a gouge, or a ticketter pressing firmly on the top surface, several strokes are made from one end of the scraper to the other (photo 4).

PHOTO TWO: scraper held at 90⁰ to the stone

PHOTO THREE: scraper rubbed flat on stone

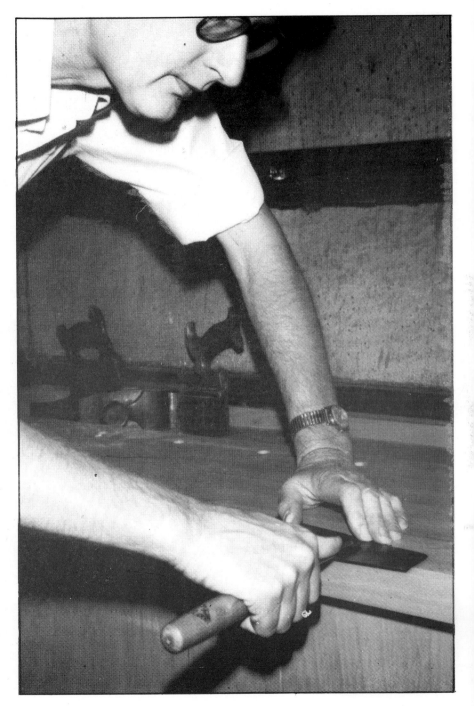

PHOTO FOUR (on previous page):
back of gouge rubbing the length of
scraper's face

The next stage is to hold the scraper upright on the bench as in photo 5 and, gripping it securely, press it hard on the bench. To prevent the corners of the scraper digging into the hand, cover the top edge with your apron. Hold the gouge slightly out of square and, applying a fair amount of pressure, bring up the gouge smartly and at the same time give a slight dragging action by pulling the hand away from the face of the scraper. This will put a better burr on the edge. Repeat this two or three times and each time incline the gouge a little further out of square until it is about 80° to the face of the scraper. All four long edges of the scraper are sharpened in the same way.

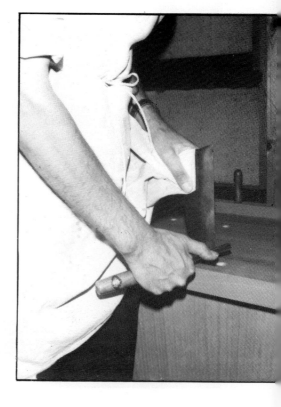

PHOTO FIVE: turning up the burr

PHOTO SIX: scraper
removing fine shavings

The scraper is used by grasping it between the fingers and thumbs of both hands and inclining it at about 60° away from the body. It is then pushed away from the operator to remove fine shavings (photo 6). There is one minor drawback to using the scraper; it heats up without warning and can burn the thumbs. The thinner the scraper, the more quickly it heats up.

The wood must now be thoroughly smoothed with abrasive paper and most polishers use garnet paper in preference to glass paper. It is slightly more expensive but longer lasting. Abrasive paper ceases to cut, not because its cutting particles are blunt, but because they are clogged with dust. Tap the paper sharply against the edge of the bench at intervals to dislodge the dust and the paper will resume cutting.

TWO Stains and staining

WE must now consider what is to be the final colour of our piece and how to achieve it.

It may be asked: why should we want to stain wood? There are several reasons. Firstly stain enriches the grain and brings out the figuring. Secondly several different varieties of one type of wood may have been used in our example and we want all these varieties to be finally one uniform colour. Thirdly our piece may be a table with a Cuban mahogany top, Honduras mahogany framing and beech legs. The two latter woods must be made to match the top and this can only be achieved by staining.

Having selected the colour, we must now choose our type of stain. Water stains are the easiest to use and have much to recommend them, though they do have the disadvantage of raising the grain and causing the wood to feel rough. The action of glass paper is to crush and bruise the fibres of the grain and the water in the stain causes the fibres to swell, hence the rough feeling. It is overcome by first sponging the wood lightly with warm water prior to staining. Let the wood dry thoroughly and paper it smooth. If the grain came up very rough it would be as well to damp it a second time and again glasspaper it. The stain can now be applied without further raising of the grain.

Always use a new piece of fine grade abrasive paper for this purpose and start by papering at a slight angle to the grain. This will ensure that the raised fibres are cut off clean and not just crushed flat only to stand up again when the stain is applied.

Finish by sanding in the direction of the grain in the usual manner.

Spirit stains are made by dissolving one ounce of spirit soluble powder in a pint of meths. This will give a strong mixture which can be instantly diluted with meths if required. Various coloured powders are readily obtainable from polish suppliers. The powder is dissolved more quickly by frequently shaking the bottle. The stain is decanted into a clean bottle and any sediment thrown away. If bottles of spirit red, yellow, green and black are made up then by careful mixing most colours can be obtained. The disadvantage of spirit stains is that they dry quickly and the work must be gone over speedily to keep the edges 'live' and thereby prevent parts of the work from being stained twice. Spirit stains do not raise the grain.

A very attractive colour can be imparted to oak, particularly English oak, by fuming with 0.880 ammonia. The number refers to the specific gravity and is the strongest available. The work is placed in a sealed cabinet or room, drawers are pulled slightly out and any doors are opened. Several saucers of ammonia are placed around the work and the cabinet is then tightly closed. If the cabinet is fitted with a window it will be possible to see after a few hours how the colour is developing and whether the desired shade has been attained. In a small cabinet where a window is not practicable a hole may be bored in the side and a protruding wooden plug fitted. The plug, being made from the same wood as the article being fumed, is withdrawn at intervals so that the colour can be checked.

It may happen that one piece of wood has darkened sufficiently while another is still light. The work is removed from the cupboard and two coats of white french polish are brushed on the dark wood to prevent further fuming. The piece is returned to the cupboard where the ammonia will continue to darken the unpolished parts. The advantage of fuming is that it does not raise the grain.

To test whether a piece of wood will fume, it should be planed, then placed over the open mouth of the ammonia bottle and within a short while the wood should change colour. Although mahogany can be fumed, this process is usually confined to oak.

Some of the commoner water stains are:

Bichromate of potash — 2ozs of crystals dissolved in a pint of water, applied with a brush to either oak or mahogany. This must be done in daylight where there is a free circulation of air to assist the chemical action.

Mahogany crystals — dissolved in water will not only darken mahogany but will stain other woods, eg beech the colour of mahogany.

Burnt sienna — dissolved in stale beer is a good mahogany stain. The sugar in the beer prevents fading. Burnt sienna is readily available from polish houses, the second ingredient should be obtained locally.

Vandyke brown — mixed into a thin paste with ammonia and thinned with water as required will make a good walnut stain. If a little Bismarck brown is added, this stain will be very suitable for oak. These two stains should be strained through an old stocking.

12

Permanganate of potash — 1oz to 1pint of water is sometimes advised as an inexpensive stain, particularly where large areas such as floors are to be stained. It has a purple colour when first applied, it soon turns brown but the colour is apt to fade. Furthermore if applied with an ordinary paint brush it rots the bristles. Apart from its low cost this stain has nothing to recommend it.

The following spirit stains will provide most of the required tones:

Mahogany — spirit red with the addition of a little spirit black.

Walnut — spirit red and spirit yellow with a little black to darken it.

Oak — spirit black and an almost equal amount of spirit red. If a light oak is required, a little spirit green may be added.

There is a certain amount of experimenting to be done to achieve the right colour and it is advisable to try the stains on pieces of scrap from the job in hand.

Having obtained the desired colour, mix up rather more stain than is needed. It is better to have a surplus than to run out part way through, because a second mixture may have a different colour from the first.

Oil stains having a white spirit base can be bought from polish houses in the following colours: light, medium and Jacobean oak, walnut and mahogany. They do not raise the grain and dry sufficiently slowly to enable the beginner to stain a sizeable job and keep all edges 'live'. The clear colours do not obscure the grain and they do not fade. More than one coat of stain can be applied if a deeper stain is required. If the stain is too strong the addition of a little white spirit will dilute it.

Recently in response to many requests for a stain to give new pine furniture an appearance of age, one polish house has developed an oil stain entitled 'weathered pine'. Judicious use of this stain will enable new furniture to harmonise with really old pieces. The stain has a pale golden tinge and imparts a faint grey effect in the grain. It can be thinned with white spirit to reduce the greyness if required. The work can be stained twice if further colour is desired. Keep the stain well shaken during use.

If the pine surface is to be subjected to hard usage such as in a kitchen it should be stained as necessary and the stain allowed to dry and lightly sanded. Bar Top lacquer to which 20% thinners has been added is brushed on, allowed to harden, then gently sanded and a second coat of lacquer applied. This lacquer is colourless and will withstand hot water, alcohol and steam from cooking.

THREE Wax polishing

THIS method of finishing is very simple and good results can be obtained even by the beginner. The polish, consisting of beeswax and turpentine, could not be plainer and its method of application is very straightforward.

Although mahogany, walnut or oak may all be wax polished, it is generally agreed that oak benefits most from waxing. The mellow sheen resulting from frequent applications of wax seems to suit oak better than the brilliance of french polish. Furthermore a table top which has been waxed will withstand the heat from hot dishes far better than a french polished one. Any accidental damage that does occur can soon be rectified by further waxing.

Although wax polish can be made by dissolving shredded wax in turpentine so that the polish has a consistency of soft butter it

is better to buy ready made polish from a trade house. The ingredients are of the best quality and each tin will be as good as the last. Silicone polishes are not recommended, as silicones may damage the original finish. Delicately perfumed polishes may make the room scented but they won't be any better for the furniture.

Wood to be waxed is prepared in the usual way by glasspapering and staining. The pores of the wood are then sealed by brushing on two coats of white french polish. When dry the surface is smoothed with fine garnet paper to remove any little pimples or imperfections, and the ensuing dust is then carefully brushed off.

The application of the white french polish serves two purposes. Firstly wax polish is not an effective barrier against

15

the ingress of dirt and over the course of years grime can penetrate the film of wax and dirty the surface of the wood. This dirt can only be cleaned off after first removing all the old polish. Brushing on two coats of white french polish after staining will prevent dirt from entering the wood and if the wax finish becomes soiled it can be washed off with white spirit leaving the wood quite clean.

The second reason for using french polish is that it seals the open pores of the grain and ensures a more rapid build up of a wax film. If the wood were left unsealed the wax would sink into the surface to be polished and many waxings would be needed to achieve a good shine.

It is important to spread the polish evenly and thinly over the work and this may be achieved either by using a rag or a shoe brush. Having done this, a second rag is used to bring up a good shine and finally a clean duster is vigorously rubbed with the grain to give the final brightness. The process should be repeated daily until a beautiful mellow finish is obtained. Unlike varnish which lies on top of the wood, a wax polish is actually in the wood and it is the wood itself which glows.

For light oak, a pale coloured wax will give a good finish without darkening the wood to any great extent. On dark oak a special dark wax is used with good effect. The dark polish sinks into the open pores of the grain to highlight its beauty. Figured oak looks particularly well when polished with dark polish. Old work which has become dirty through neglect can be improved by washing away old wax and furniture cream with

warm water and toilet soap. Care
must be taken not to be too liberal
in the use of water and to wipe
dry when all the dirt has been
removed. The wood is allowed to
dry naturally and slowly before it
is waxed.

FOUR Oil polishing

THIS method of finishing is particularly suitable for dining table tops because it is much more durable than wax polish or french polish. It is not spoiled by water being spilled on it and neither is it blistered by heat. The only reason why oil polishing is not popular today is because of the labour involved. The materials used could not be simpler — linseed oil and friction! Some polishers will advise raw linseed oil while others swear by the boiled variety and there are many who prefer a mixture of both. Whichever variation is selected by the polisher, the method of application is the same. The preparation of the wood follows the usual pattern, namely scraping and glasspapering until a perfectly smooth surface is obtained, followed by staining to the desired colour, or possibly a shade lighter. The application at intervals of linseed oil has a darkening effect and over a period of time light oak will darken almost to a Jacobean colour. It will also bring out the beauty of the grain in a way unequalled by any other method. Oil polishing consists of rubbing in linseed oil and polishing with a clean duster. The rubbing in of the oil and subsequent polishing is continued until the desired shine is reached. The more vigorous rubbing the work is given, the better it will shine and it may take some weeks before the desired result is obtained. The final effect is not a brilliant finish such as french polish but a dull sheen which is similar to a waxed finish.

When Cuban mahogany was first imported into the UK it was usually polished with red oil made by steeping four ounces of bruised alkanet root in a pint of raw linseed oil. This gave the wood a rich red appearance. At a later date when Honduras mahogany was more commonly used, plain linseed oil was used to polish it and such old pieces have matured to a most desirable honey colour. Alkanet root is now no longer obtainable, but a similar effect can be achieved by dissolving Bismarck brown in linseed oil.

Oiling consists of applying the oil to the wood with a rag sparingly and rubbing it well in. It is a mistake to be too liberal and to flood the work with oil in the hope that a polish will be gained more quickly. This will only result in a sticky mess and be most unsatisfactory.

If a large table top is to be polished some oil is rubbed well into it. It is then polished by wrapping some felt or green baize round a brick or some other weighty object and polishing the wood until it is quite dry. The reason for using a brick is to save the polisher from having to apply pressure to the flannel. All his energy can then be directed to keeping the brick moving! There is no denying that a great deal of energy is expended and at first there is very little to show for one's efforts. The first rubbing will slightly darken the wood but will produce very little gloss. By continuing the process a few times a gloss will appear and after a month or so a most attractive and durable finish will be obtained.

How does the polisher know when the polishing is finished? Well he doesn't because an oiled piece will always take a little more oil and a lot more friction. That is why oil polishing cannot be done commercially, it takes far too much time. Also there is another

drawback. On account of the time
and effort needed, oil polishing of
anything but plain work is out of
the question.

Intricate carvings and mouldings
can be oil finished but the time
needed would be excessive.
However, a few rubs of oil will
greatly enhance the colour of the
wood and reveal richness of grain.
It is no wonder that so much
Cuban mahogany was finished
with oil before the advent of
french polishing.

FIVE French polishing, bodying up and spiriting off

OF all the finishes available to the cabinetmaker there is nothing to equal skilfully applied french polish. The full beauty of the wood is shown to its best advantage and the brilliance of this finish reflects the figuring and contrast of the grain. Unlike varnish or a sprayed-on finish there is no thickness in french polish. It does not lie on top like paint but is actually in the pores of the wood so that its thickness is less than that of a cigarette paper.

The polish and its method of application was developed in France by the Martin brothers more than two hundred years ago. It was introduced into England in 1815. The original formula and method of application used by the Martins remained a secret which died with them. The polish used today is probably very similar to the original, although there are now several different varieties of colour. The basis of all french polishes is shellac and methylated spirits. Shellac is made from lac, a resinous substance found on the branches of several varieties of trees in Assam and Bengal. The female insect, known as the red bug, lays eggs in the bark of the trees from which a resinous substance oozes and hardens on the twigs. These twigs are then broken off, dried in the sun and the resinous substance pounded off the twigs. This is known as seed lac and when melted, collected and cooled is called lump lac. It is melted in cotton bags and the filtered substance flows over planks where it cools into thin flakes and is known as shellac.

The polish is made by dissolving three pounds of shellac in a gallon of methylated spirits (known as a 'three pound cut'). A heavier grade of polish for application by brush has five pounds of shellac to a gallon of meths ('five pound cut'). Although polish is now sold in litres, the usual quantity being five litres, the description 'three pound cut' is still used.

It is strongly advised that polish is bought from a trade house, because only the best ingredients are used and the quality is consistently high.

There are several varieties:

Button polish – brown in colour with a slight yellowish tinge.

Brown polish – made from orange shellac and used principally on mahogany. It is usually referred to simply as 'polish'.

Garnet polish – made from garnet shellac is dark but more transparent than either button or brown polish. It gives old mahogany a desired warmth.

White polish – made from shellac bleached by acid which is then kept in damp sawdust. It is dried carefully before being dissolved in meths. It may have a life of two years and should therefore not be bought in large quantities. There is no obvious sign that it has deteriorated until it is applied to the wood. It will then be found that several days later it is still soft. Stripping and repolishing with fresh polish is the only remedy and the perished polish should be thrown away. White polish is used on light woods such as oak and ash.

Transparent white polish – is made from shellac that has been bleached twice and is used where darkening of the wood, as in marquetry work is to be avoided.

Red polish – used for mahogany where additional red shade is required.

PHOTO SEVEN: wadding 10in x 5in

Black polish – for ebony or wood that has been ebonised.

P.S.L. polish — this is made from pure stick lac, hence the initials. Its colour bears a resemblance to that of port wine. It gives a hard finish, a brilliant shine and is consequently ideal for polishing pianos. In fact before pianos were spray finished this polish was known as 'P.S.L. piano polish'.

Imperva polish — This is a shellac polish which has been specially treated to give it a greater degree of resistance than conventional french polish to water, alcohol and heat. The writer has seen wood polished with 'Imperva' in exterior situations where it has been subjected to rain, snow and fog and has remained unmarked. It combines the beauty of shellac with the durability of other finishes.

PHOTO EIGHT: wadding folded in half

23

Although hot plates and alcohol cannot be left on an 'Imperva' surface for a considerable time with impunity, such a surface will stand up to a great deal of punishment without marking.

The method of application differs slightly from other french polishes and this is described on page 32.

The polisher applies polish to the wood by means of a rubber and the photographs show how one is made. Photo 7 shows a piece of wadding approximately 10in x 5in. It is folded in half (photo 8) and finally three of the corners are folded in (photo 9). When folded, the wadding is covered with a clean soft white rag. The rag must be lint free and seam free and of a fine texture. Well washed linen handkerchiefs are most suitable but if these are not available, a supply of white rag can be bought from a polish house together with wadding.

The rag is carefully folded over the front of the rubber (Fig 2). It is then folded as in Fig 3 to preserve the rubber's pointed shape and finally the two remaining corners are folded in and twisted

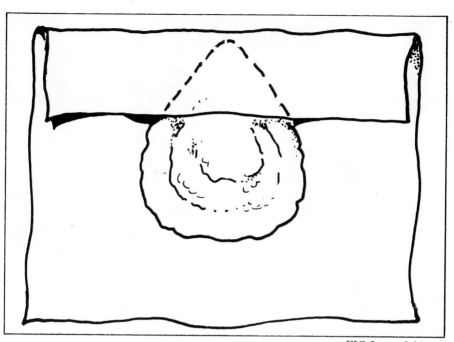

FIG 2: rag folded
over point of rubber

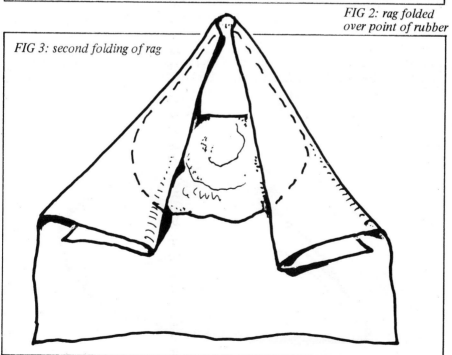

FIG 3: second folding of rag

PHOTO NINE: corners of wadding folded in

so that the final shape is as Fig 4.

Before polishing can begin the rubber must be charged with polish; beginners are apt to err on the generous side and make the rubber too wet. It is a good plan to cut a V-shaped notch down the length of the polish bottle cork so that the flow of polish can be regulated. The rag covering is undone and sufficient polish is poured into the wadding so that when the rag covering is gathered up again and the rubber pressed into the palm of the hand the polish will ooze through.

Because old rubbers work better than new ones, they should be kept in airtight screw topped glass jars. If a rubber is not being used for some time it is advisable to put a few drops of meths in the

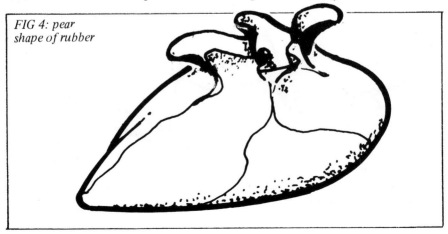

FIG 4: pear shape of rubber

*PHOTO TEN:
shaped sticks
to remove
excess
filler from
mouldings*

jar to keep the rubber soft. If a
rubber does go hard, it should be
thrown away and a fresh one
made. Do not keep either rubbers
or french polish in tins, because
the meths will eat into the tinplate
and ruin both rubber and polish.

Keep rubbers which have been
used for different polishes in
separate jars and also keep spirit
rubbers in their own jar.

The first operation of polishing
is filling the grain. Without this
the polisher would have to put in
a lot of time and polish filling the
open pores of the wood, especially
when polishing hungry woods
such as oak or ash. A filler
composed of whiting and turpentine, coloured to match the work
in hand, is used to choke the open
grain and thus speed up the
polishing.

Various coloured fillers are
obtainable from polish houses and
it is not worth trying to make
one's own. The filler is picked up
on a piece of coarse rag and forced
into the open pores by rubbing it
across the grain. It will appear dull
as it dries out and the surplus is
removed by rubbing across the
grain. Finally a clean rag is used to
rub it with the grain. Excess filler
which lodges in quirks and
mouldings is removed with the aid
of specially shaped sticks (photo
10).

The filler is then allowed to
harden overnight. It is dusted off
and rubbed with a rag moistened
with raw linseed oil. The oil is well
rubbed in and it gives the work a
clean appearance. Failure to use
oil at this stage would leave the
wood looking slightly muddy. The
work is allowed to stand overnight
to let it harden and then it is
lightly papered down.

If the wood is close grained its

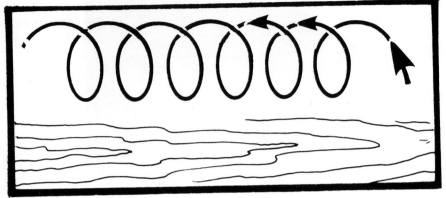

grain can be filled with 'sealer D', a shellac based filler. This has two great advantages, the white coloured liquid can be used on wood of any colour and polishing can begin 20 minutes after application.

We are now in a position to start polishing. The rubber is charged with polish and is worked across the grain in continuous straight strokes. When the whole area has been covered the rubber is then worked along the grain. The polish soon soaks into the wood and may cause the rubber to drag, if so recharge with polish and carry on. Linseed oil is not used during this operation.

When using the rubber, never let it stand still on the work or it will damage the soft layer of shellac beneath it. Do not have any creases or folds on the face of your rubber as this will prevent

the even application of polish. A slight whistling sound can often be heard when a fold is present. Glide the rubber smoothly on to one end of the work and off the other to avoid building up ridges of polish. Keep the fingernail short so they do not inadvertently scratch the soft polish and don't allow accumulations of old polish to build up on the fingers. A piece is sure to flake off and become embedded in a newly polished surface.

The next stage is bodying up. The rubber is used in a series of overlapping circles as shown in Fig 5 and alternated with figures of eight across the grain as in Fig 6. When first charged the rubber is used with a light pressure which is increased as the rubber dries out.

If it tends to drag, the tip of a finger is dipped in raw linseed oil and wiped across the face of the

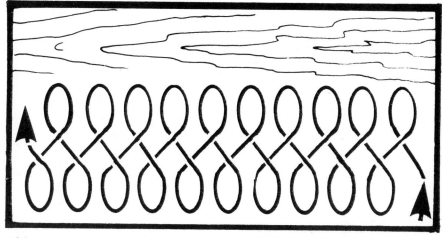

rubber to act as a lubricant. Use as little oil as possible, for at the final stage all oil has to be removed. The advantage of polishing in overlapping circles and figures of eight is that it helps to achieve a more even body of polish over the work. Beginners tend to apply more pressure to the outward loops of their circles than their inner loops and semicircular ridges may appear. With experience the pressure on the rubber is even so there will be no ridges. If such unevenness is noticed it can usually be removed by working the rubber in straight sweeps along the grain.

When bodying care should be taken not to go over the same area twice in quick succession. If the rubber is passed over a surface that has just been polished it will tend to tear up the soft lac and damage it. Test the softness of the polish by gently touching with a clean knuckle. If slightly sticky, allow it to harden for a few minutes before applying more polish.

Beginners usually find that the centre of a panel has a better polish than the edge. When they see a shine appearing they tend to concentrate on that area and also in the beginning they find corners difficult. If edges and corners are looked after, the centres will look after themselves.

Bodying is continued by re-charging the rubber and applying oil when necessary until the grain is full; the work is set aside until the following day. Do not leave the work standing in the direct glare of strong sunlight as this may cause tiny blisters to form.

By the following day the polish will have sunk a little and may feel

29

a trifle gritty. A piece of fine, worn garnet paper is held between the fingers (photo 11) and, rubbing in the direction of the grain, any slight imperfections are smoothed away. The paper held thus enables the polisher to have a better feel of the work than if a cork glasspapering block were used. The work is carefully dusted off and bodying is continued until the grain is filled. Having ensured that the grain is nicely full, the rubber is charged with 75 per cent polish and 25 per cent meths by first pouring in the polish and then topping up with spirit. Work in straight sweeps with the grain and only use the merest quantity of oil if absolutely necessary.

The next time the rubber needs charging, use half polish and half meths; using a thinned mixture will refine the surface in readiness for the finishing touch — called

spiriting off.

Spiriting off removes all the linseed oil, smooths out the shellac and burnishes it to that clear brilliance typical of a quality french polished surface. It is a stage where care and skill must be exercised, for a heavy-handed approach can wash away the polish that has been so laboriously applied.

A new rubber is made, similar to the bodying rubber except that the spirit rubber has three or four coverings of rag on it. Charge it only with meths in such an amount that, when all the coverings are gathered up and the sole of the rubber is applied to the face, it just feels cold. It must not feel wet, otherwise it will wash

PHOTO ELEVEN: holding garnet paper between fingers

PHOTO TWELVE: polish applied to moulding with bear-hair mop

away the shellac. With a light touch, glide along the grain from one end of the work to the other (photo 12). Here again, do not go over the same ground twice in rapid succession. After a while a 'tide mark' will appear round the edge of the rubber; this is linseed oil being lifted out of the shellac. As the rubber dries the outer rag covering is removed to expose a clean face and a moister one. Continue spiriting until all the oil is removed and a brilliantly clear smooth surface appears. By this time the final covering on the rubber will have been reached.

If only one cover were used on the spiriting rubber, the rag would soon contain so much oil that instead of removing the oil the rubber would re-distribute it. When this occurs, the polish in the wake of the rubber is brilliant at first, but dull parallel lines soon

appear and the shellac film does not clear. The remedy is to keep the rag cover clean.

When using Imperva polish the work is stained and the grain filled in the usual way. Although it is similar in appearance to transparent white it is advisable to make up a separate rubber and keep it solely for use with this polish.

Charge the rubber with polish and work it across the grain and then along the grain in the usual way. Bodying up now follows working the rubber in circular, figure of eight movements and straight sweeps along the grain. Do not use raw linseed oil on the face of the rubber as a lubricant. If a lubricant is necessary then a small quantity of white oil may be used. It is however better if polishing can be accomplished without oil. The entire process of bodying and spiriting off should be completed in the one day. The reason is that if the work is bodied and left to harden until the following day, 'Imperva's' resistance to alcohol will prevent subsequent applications from softening the first. In these circumstances the second application might not entirely amalgamate with the first and a perfect finish might not be achieved.

Another method of finishing, which was favoured by German polishers when polishing pianos, involves dilute sulphuric acid. Special piano polish made from the purest shellac is used in the normal way to body-up. A little sulphuric acid is slowly poured into water in small quantities to form a dilute solution of one part acid to twelve parts of water. The water must never be poured into the acid. A rag is dipped into the solution and then wiped all over the work. The dilute acid is rubbed into the work with the palm of the hand so that the surface has a uniformly smeary appearance. The acid is used to lift out the linseed oil. A 'pounce bag' containing Vienna chalk is shaken over the palm of the hand and a little chalk at a time is rubbed into the work. The film of acid will disappear as dusting and rubbing continues and in a short time the whole area will be dry and bright, with no trace of oil. The shellac will have been burnished brilliantly by the finest polisher of all — the human skin.

The acid finish should only be attempted by experienced polishers, for if the grain is not perfectly filled, Vienna chalk will be visible in the open pores and the whole effect spoiled.

Keep the dilute acid in a glass stoppered bottle, clearly labelled and out of the reach of children. The Vienna chalk (which is not the same as french chalk) must be kept in a warm dry place because it readily picks up dampness which makes it useless.

A popular finish at the present time is the eggshell finish. Having achieved a bright french polished finish the work is allowed to harden for a couple of days. With a soft brush or felt block, some fine pumice powder is worked in the direction of the grain. The brush is damped and worked in straight lines. Finally it is dried off with a chamois leather and rubbed with a dry rag also along the grain.

SIX Dry shining

ONCE the art of french polishing has been acquired dry shining will present no difficulty. This finish can be used on the insides of wardrobes, bookcases and writing desks where a high polish is not required but a protective finish is needed. It can be done expeditiously and therefore cheaply and it closes the grain thereby preventing it being clogged with dust or finger marked. It also gives a certain amount of finish, which wood left in the white does not have.

The wood is bodied without any preliminary filling of the grain and less care is needed than when a full polish is to be obtained. The rubber is charged in the normal way and wiped over the wood in the usual circular movements. A full body is not necessary, just a few strokes of the rubber will be sufficient to seal the open pores in the grain. Linseed oil is not used and the rubber may tend to drag as it dries out. If it were lubricated with oil the spirit rubber would be needed to lift out the oil. Ultimately the whole process of french polishing would have been gone through, thereby defeating our object.

Having achieved a sufficient body, the rubber is charged rather more fully than usual and is wiped over the work from one end to the other. It is worked back and forth until dry but the polish is allowed to harden before going over the same ground again.

SEVEN Glazing

GLAZING may be said to be an imitation of french polishing for it is a means of producing a good finish quickly and easily. The finish is. however, not as good or as long lasting as a properly french polished finish. But it has particular uses.

Glaze is often used on fretwork which is too intricate to permit a rubber to work into all the corners and edges. Carvings and mouldings are often glazed for the same reason. Other jobs may be glazed because a good finish has to be achieved rapidly, and durability may not be important.

Glaze, sometimes known as 'slake', 'telegraph' or 'lightning', is made by dissolving 6oz gum banzoin in methylated spirit. It is usual to buy it ready-made. If you do make your own, allow the mixture to stand for several days and after the benzoin has dissolved the solution should be strained through muslim to clear it of impurities. Glaze improves with keeping.

Glaze can be applied to tricky carvings and mouldings with a brush but it is more usual to apply it with the rubber. Body-up the work with french polish until the stage is reached where you are using a mixture of half polish and half-spirit. The glaze rubber should be a little wetter than the polishing rubber, but not soaking wet. Now with a very little pressure from the rubber the glaze should be laid on. Go over the work lightly with the grain. Wait until the surface is dry before you go over the same place again. Several coats may be applied until a satisfactory finish is obtained.

The appearance of glaze can be improved by lightly working a rubber charged solely with spirits over it. Be light with your touch or you may find you have washed away all the glaze.

Glaze is not suitable for wide surfaces because it is so difficult to apply without forming ridges on the polished surface. If ridges do appear they can be carefully removed with a swab rubber, moistened with meths and the merest touch of linseed oil on it. Go over the glazed surface very lightly and change the direction of the rubber, just as you do in spiriting-off.

A swab rubber is made by folding a piece of clean rag into the shape of an ordinary rubber but without using wadding in it.

The advantage of glaze is that it can be used where a polishing rubber cannot always reach. Although it is expensive it can save time and this can mean money.

A branch of my family who were undertakers used glaze to polish coffins. When coffins were made to measure out of oak or elm there was very little time allowed for polishing, so glaze was used to speed the process. The coffin would be supported by two battens screwed at a suitable distance apart on a wooden bench. This enabled the polisher to work on one side of the coffin, then lift it off the battens, turn it so that the other side or one of the ends was uppermost and carry on working without having to wait for the first side to dry or harden.

The first step was to bring up the figure of the grain by rubbing raw linseed oil well into the wood. Then the grain was filled with a filler made from whiting and turpentine mixed into a stiff paste. The filler had to be stained to match the wood: ochre for oak;

ochre and venetian red for elm.

A large rubber was made up and charged with french polish and wiped over the coffin two or three times until it had a fair body of polish on it. With a very fine glasspaper it was smoothed down, dusted off and a coat of naptha varnish applied. As soon as this was dry it was smoothed down with another rubber of polish. Gradually the polish would be thinned down with meths. Another coat of varnish would probably complete the job though if there was time (and money) the lid had a little extra attention. The varnish was sometimes smoothed down by rubbing over with polish then finishing off with glaze or possibly spiriting-off. Wood naptha would be used as a solvent for the polish and the varnish instead of meths. This method would put quite a good finish on a coffin.

With elm coffins the plinth and moulding were often coloured to look like mahogany. This effect was achieved by using coloured polish. When time and money were short a couple of coats of quick-drying varnish sufficed. But whatever the finish, we never had a customer who came back and complained!

EIGHT Re~polishing

LTHOUGH a french polished surface retains its beautiful appearance for many years, it may, through accident, misuse or neglect, have to be repolished. Antiques are often in need of repair and re-polishing and when engaged on this sort of work one comes across some unusual 'restorations' and 'improvements'.

The work must proceed methodically and in an orderly manner. Brass handles, locks and other fittings are carefully removed and put safely away in suitable containers. Any mouldings that unscrew from the back are removed and given mating marks so that they are replaced in the correct position. Having removed doors, drawers and taken apart any pieces that are screwed together, the work is much easier to handle and examine.

It may be that after washing with toilet soap and warm water the old polish will be seen to be sound and in good condition and repolishing can proceed. If this is so it can be carefully rubbed down with no 1 wire wool, followed by fine garnet paper held between the fingers. All traces of dust are wiped away and polishing is begun with a rubber charged with half polish and half meths. Thinned polish softens the original shellac film and helps the new polish to take more readily to the old. Bodying continues with full strength polish to build up a good body, after which the polish is diluted and spirited off in the usual manner.

In the event of the old polish being crazed, it will be necessary to remove it altogether. On plain surfaces the steel cabinet scraper will be invaluable. It will however, need to be sharpened frequently because old french polish can be fearfully hard. Another method is to place the surface to be stripped in a vertical position, to sweep a meths soaked rag over it and then set the moistened area alight at the bottom. The old polish is burned off leaving the wood clean and dry ready for polishing. Burning off should not be attempted in a wooden shed or where there is an accumulation of shavings on the floor.

Where there are mouldings or carvings, a stripper should be used and the manufacturers' directions carefully followed, particularly as regards neutralising the stripper. Where the old polish has been entirely removed, the surface is treated as new work and is stained, filled and polished in a similar manner. It may happen that the corner of a table top is broken and has to be repaired by letting in a new piece of wood . Here we have the old and the new side by side and one has to be blended with the other. The new piece is stained to match, but as bodying proceeds it is noticed that the repair is lighter than it should be. To overcome this a little spirit stain of the appropriate colour is added to some french polish and brushed over the light area with a bear hair mop (Fig 7). When the colour is sufficiently deep, bodying is continued using normal unstained polish.

Sometimes it happens that in glasspapering in readiness for repolishing a corner is rubbed through and unstained wood shows up. Stain applied to the corner runs down the edge rather than stay where it is needed. In these cases add up to 10 per cent polish to the stain and brush it on

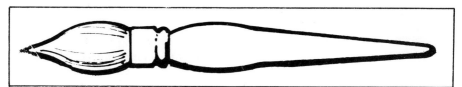

the bare corner with a small artist's brush. The polish binds the stain and retains it in the required position.

The tops of occasional tables which have been in strong sunlight are inclined to fade and the polish deteriorates. There is no difficulty in removing the old polish and restaining, but problems can occur where there are boxwood stringings or inlays of light coloured wood.

How does one stain walnut or mahogany without darkening the lighter woods? The answer lies in a keen eye and a steady hand. Using a clean artist's brush, white polish is applied to the stringing and other parts which are not to be stained. The polish is allowed to go hard when it will act as a mask. Stain is applied to the whole, but will only colour the exposed areas. When the stain has dried out the complete top is polished with white polish.

When the surface will stand repolishing it is advisable to check what finish has been used previously. It might very well be french polish, but varnish could have been employed or even cellulose. Oak looks best when waxed but is frequently varnished. Experiments are carried out on an inconspicuous part. Put a little meths on the finish and if after a few minutes the polish has softened then french polish was used. Meths will not affect either varnish or cellulose. If no softening occurs then scrape the finish with the edge of a chisel. A yellow shaving indicates varnish was used whereas white powder will scrape off if the finish was cellulose. French polish should not be applied on top of cellulose or varnish.

When a panelled door is made,

41

FIG 8: point of rubber polishing into corner of panelled door

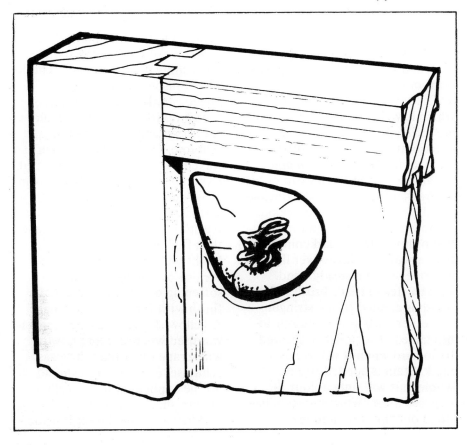

it is far easier if the panel is bodied up before the door is assembled. When the framing has been glued the final processes are gone through fairly easily. In a repolishing job it is not possible to dismantle the door to facilitate polishing and this is where the *point* of the rubber comes in. Fig 8 shows the point being used to polish the mouldings and corner of a panelled door. The same technique is employed when polishing the corners of cock beaded drawer fronts. The forefinger is placed over the point and the rubber is drawn along the mouldings out of the corner.

When mouldings are so intricate that a rubber cannot reach into all the quirks, the polish is best applied with a bear hair mop (photo 13). This is also the best way to tackle turned or reeded legs. On the other hand, cabriole legs are usually polished with the rubber. By not applying too much polish at a time a brush will give a satisfactory finish.

Mention is often made of revivers. Nothing can be done to a badly damaged surface short of stripping and repolishing but if the surface is still sound, then reviving is possible. Most revivers are a success because they clear away all deposits of grease, wax furniture creams and dirt. If there is a large accumulation of dirt it should be washed off with toilet soap and warm water and then dried. Provided there is not a great deal of old furniture cream to be cleaned off, a reviver made from two parts vinegar, two parts raw linseed oil, two parts white spirit

PHOTO THIRTEEN: spiriting off.
Note correct way of holding rubber

43

PHOTO THIRTEEN: spiriting off.
Note correct way of holding rubber

and one part meths well shaken up will prove beneficial. Another good reviewer is made from equal parts of raw linseed oil, vinegar and turps.

Where there are small pin holes, or small pieces of veneer are missing, the damage can often be made good by using hard stopping or *beaumontage.* Sticks of different colours are available from polish houses and their colours should be the same as the finished colour or slightly darker because the stopping does not take stain. The work is set horizontally while the stopping is held against the point of a hot steel knitting needle directly above the place to be filled. Stopping is dropped into the blemish until it is slightly overfilled. After a few minutes it will have set and the surplus is then flushed off with a wide chisel. Although stopping cannot

be stained it can be polished and after polishing the blemish should be imperceptible.

Bruises. Most old pieces of furniture suffer from dents and bruises. Many of these bruises are time honoured scars and should be left as they are. In reproduction furniture such brusies are often deliberately inflicted to give the appearance of age, a process known as 'distressing'. There are occasions, however, when it is desirable to take out the bruise and there are two methods of approach.

The first method is to fill the hollow with methylated spirits. The spirit bottle is now placed in a safe position well out of the way before setting alight to the spirit in the bruised area. Just before the meths is all burned away it must be blown out. If the bruise is a deep one it may be necessary to have two or three burnings.

A word of caution; when meths is burning the flame is almost invisible so be careful you don't start an unwanted fire.

The second method uses steam to swell the wood fibres. The dent is filled with water which is alllowed to soak in for ten minutes or so. If the film of polish is unbroken it must be pricked through with a needle in several places to let the water penetrate. Now soak a piece of wadding in water and place it on the bruise. Heat up a large soldering iron or similar piece of metal and place it firmly on the wadding to raise steam and thereby swell the bruised area. It may be necessary to repeat the process to bring the bruise level. Allow the work to thoroughly dry before

glasspapering smooth in readiness for staining.

It sometimes happens that a damaged area is so badly broken or worm eaten that it has to be cut out and replaced. A less visible repair can be made if old wood is used rather than new, especially if the piece to be let in has a similar grain pattern to that which it is replacing. Usually, however, this ideal situation does not arise and the polisher has to blend in the repair as best he can. By skilful use of stains the new wood is brought to the same colour as the old. Then using a bird's wing feather dipped in spirit black stain the prominent features of the grain can be drawn in. If spirit black is not to hand a good black stain for this purpose can be made by placing a handful of rusty nails in a pint of vinegar. Agitate the bottle at intervals and the stain will be ready for use after two or three days. The stain is allowed to dry and if necessary the edges of the applied 'grain' are lightly smudged with fine worn glasspaper to give a more natural appearance. Dust off and brush on two coats of french polish to seal in the colour before bodying up.

It sometimes happens that after bodying, the repaired area shows up lighter in colour than the rest of the work. Judicious use of spirit stains will rectify matters. For example to darken a mahogany repair, mix some spirit black with Bismark brown, add to some french polish and starting from the outside and working towards the centre brush the coloured polish over the light area. After bringing the colour to the right depth seal it in by brushing on two coats of ordinary uncoloured polish and continue polishing in the usual manner.

NINE Recipes

Although ready made stains are widely used nowadays owing to their reliability and to the wide range available, the following still hold their own, partly because they are inexpensive and partly because they have never been improved upon for certain purposes. They are widely used in the trade.

Vandyke crystals give a rich brown colour, varying from a deep tone to a light shade. Ideal for oak, walnut (used weak) and occasionally for cold tones of mahogany. Also for deal or plywood to match oak or walnut.

Dissolve vandyke crystals in warm water (amount depends upon strength required). Strain through muslin and add a dash of 0.880 ammonia (ask for point eight eighty amonia). The ammonia helps to drive the stain into the grain. Keep the stain well corked after the ammonia has been added. Vandyke crystals are also sometimes known as walnut crystals.

Bichromate of potash is widely used to darken mahogany, to which it gives a somewhat cold brown tone, the depth of which can be varied according to strength. It can also be used for oak, to which it gives a slightly greenish-brown tone.

Dissolve bichromate of potash crystals in water to make a concentrated solution (ie until the water will absorb no more), bottle and dilute as required. Use in daylight. Some varieties of the same wood are more affected than others; mixed woods should therefore be avoided. It is sometimes useful after fuming to correct unevenness in tone. Both crystals and stain are deep orange in colour which bears no relation to the shade produced in the wood. Most softwoods and some hardwoods are not affected by it.

Aniline dyes are obtainable in powder form in many colours and soluble in water, methylated spirits and oil. Avoid colours which are unorthodox for woodwork. Vandyke brown is the most useful. To warm this add *a little* Bismarck brown (this is a fiery red). For a colder tone add black. Make up each stain separately and mix the liquids as required. Other colours sometimes useful are yellow, green, blue, mauve and red but use with caution as the result can be startling.

Spirit stain. Dissolve aniline spirit powder in methylated spirit (amount according to tone). Strain through muslin. Add a dessert-spoonful of french polish to each pint of stain to bind it. The stain dries rapidly, so a quick,

deft touch is needed.

Water stain. Dissolve aniline water powder in warm water (amount according to tone). Strain through muslin. Add a dessert-spoonful of hot glue and a dash of vinegar. Use warm.

Oil stain. Dissolve aniline oil powder in turpentine. Heat in hot water (not naked flame). Strain through muslin. Add a dessert-spoonful of gold size. Order the aniline dye in accordance with the liquid with which it is to be mixed — spirit, water or oil.

Ammonia

Generally used in fuming, but will slightly darken oak and mahogany if applied as a liquid. Use 0.880 (point eight eighty).

Fuming

Used mostly for oak, which it turns a deep and rather cold

brown. The shade may be anything from a light brown tone to almost black. Some varieties of oak take to it more than others. English, Austrian, Japanese and American white oak are all affected by it, some more than others. American red oak is the least affected of the oaks.

Prepare an airtight box or chamber and insert work and two to three saucers of 0.880 ammonia. Close up and leave until the colour required is reached. Add more ammonia if necessary.

To save opening the door, insert a dowel of the same kind of oak through a hole. Withdraw occasionally to check progress. Avoid standing over the cupboard when opening as fumes are strong. Remove all grease and glue from wood before fuming and avoid overlapping parts.

Floor stain

For a new floor the following is effective:

Dissolve vandyke crystals in 1 pint warm water. Add a good tablespoon of 0.880 ammonia. Add tablespoon of hot scotch glue. Use warm.

Or use burnt umber ground in oil. Thin with linseed oil and turps. Add a little liquid drier. When dry, rub off surface grease with coarse cloth and give coat of spirit varnish.

For a mahogany colour substitute venetian red for burnt umber.

Bleaches

Oxalic acid is used for lightening the tone of wood locally, for bleaching stains which are too dark and for taking out ink marks etc.

Dissolve 1oz oxalic acid

crystals in ½pt of hot water. Apply to work with a rag. Several applications may be needed. Wipe over with vinegar. Wash with clear water and dry.

Oxalic acid is poisonous and should be kept from the fingers. Remove all traces from the work, otherwise it may attack any subsequent finish.

For a more drastic bleach to produce the effect known as 'bleached mahogany' a powerful proprietary bleach is used on the bare wood. This will take the redness out of Honduras mahogany, leaving it almost white. It should be finished afterwards with white polish. The instructions supplied with bleach should be followed. Cuban mahogany cannot be bleached successfully.

French polishes

Orange polish. Dissolve 6oz orange shellac in 1pt methylated spirits.

Button polish. Dissolve 6oz button shellac in 1pt methylated spirits.

Garnet polish. Dissolve 6oz garnet shellac in 1pt methylated spirits.

White polish. Dissolve 6-8oz bleached shellac in 1pt methylated spirits.

Ebony polish. Dissolve ½oz aniline spirit black in 1pt of white polish. Strain through muslin. Dip in and press Reckitt's washing blue to give extra lustre.

Brush Polish. This is heavier than ordinary polish, and is made by dissolving 5lbs of shellac in a gallon of meths.

Wax polishes

Light polish. Shred bleached beeswax. Dissolve in turpentine to form a thin paste (like butter in the summertime).

Normal polish. Substitute unbleached beeswax in the above.

Brown polish. Shred unbleached beeswax. Dissolve in turpentine, making a thin paste. Add raw or burnt umber powder and stir thoroughly.

Antique (black) polish. Shred unbleached beeswax. Dissolve in turpentine, forming a thin paste. Add lamp black powder and stir thoroughly.

The dissolving of the wax in any of the above recipes can be speeded by warming the mixture in a jar of hot water. Keep it away from naked flame. Any of the polishes above can be hardened by the addition of carnauba wax. The proportion could be one part of carnauba wax to three or four of beeswax. Another way of hardening polish is to add a small amount of powdered rosin dissolved with the wax. Petrol (as used in lighters) is sometimes added to wax polish to speed up evaporation. Allow one quarter hour for the turps to evaporate before polishing.

Strippers

Household soda dissolved in hot water and used strong, then washed down afterwards, will remove french polish. It has a slight darkening tendency. Many proprietary strippers are now available which have no darkening tendency on any wood. They also have the advantage of not being so messy. All traces of caustic or alkaline strippers must be removed as they may attack any finishes subsequently applied. Wash with vinegar and clear water. Always follow manufacturer's instructions.

Polish revivers

An effective reviver can be

made by mixing equal parts of raw linseed oil, white spirit, vinegar and a half part of methylated spirits. The mixture is well shaken both before and during use. It is applied with a cotton wadding rubber well moistened with the reviver. Use it in the same way as a french polishing rubber, then dry the surface and finally polish with a clean soft duster.

Another reviver consists of equal parts of vinegar, linseed oil and methylated spirits.

If the furniture is very dirty it should first be cleaned by washing it with warm soda water, about half a cupful of soda dissolved in a gallon of water. Wipe dry and then apply the reviver. They can only be successfully used when the polished surface, though dull, is in sound condition. If the polish is blistered or crazed, a reviver will be of little value and nothing short of repolishing will be satisfactory.

Limed oak

Use a proprietary liming paste. This has merely to be rubbed into the grain. Being of a waxy nature it gives a dull eggshell gloss as the rubbing is continued. Liming paste is made with zinc white added to wax polish.

Another method is to mix whiting with water to form a thick paste and rub well into the grain. When dry rub across the grain with a brush to remove the surplus whiting and follow with a coarse rag rubbed with the grain. A couple of rubbers of french polish (white) will give an eggshell shine or white wax polish can be used.

Non-slip recipe

Floor – to prevent slipping sprinkle french chalk on the floor around the bench.

Stoppings

Beaumontage is a hard stopping for cabinet work. Proprietary sticks are available very cheaply, but if you want to make your own the recipe is: mix equal parts of beeswax and crushed rosin. Add a few flakes of brown or orange shellac. Heat in a tin and stir well together. Add powder colour to suit wood it is to match; vandyke brown for walnut and dark oak, or venetian red or red ochre for mahogany. Stir thoroughly and either keep in tin or pour out into the rounded corner of a tin lid to form into sticks. In the latter case heat a pointed iron and press the stopping against it so that the latter runs down into the hole. If kept in the tin the latter is heated and the stopping applied with a pointed matchstick.

Lubricants

For drawers — candlegrease rubbed on dry. Suitable for other working parts. Apply after polishing. Do not use oil.

Polish for turned work

Wax. Ordinary wax polish can be applied while wood is revolving in the lathe. After applying leave for several hours to allow the turps to evaporate before polishing. Carnauba wax gives a good gloss. Hold the lump wax against the revolving wood and move slowly across the work. Make a hard cloth rubber by tying a knot in fluffless cloth, press against the work and move slowly along to spread wax evenly and burnish.

Varnish. This should be brush applied with the wood stationary Use a rubbing variety and, when

thoroughly hard, burnish with
a motor car polish applied with a
rag, the work revolving at lowest
speed.

To finish oak. Two coats of
white french polish brushed on,
smoothed down when hard with
glass paper and finished with a
clear wax.

Polishing teak. It is perfectly
safe to french polish teak. The
only precaution necessary is to
begin by wiping over well with
white spirit which will remove any
free oil or grease on the surface.
Generally it is possible to omit
the filling stage as there is very
little sinkage with teak and the
grain is not coarse. Good rubber
work will soon produce a full
grain finish and this will give the
best possible bond. Work with the
rubber from the start. Do not use
oil until the surface has been
fadded, and keep the surface clean.

Alternatively apply one coat
(brushed) and an hour later fill
the grain using a mid-oak filler.
Stir well. Thin if necessary with a
little turps. Brush on a coat,
a section at a time. When the glint
goes off, which takes a minute or
so wipe off all surplus with fresh
rags. Next day paper lightly,
checking that all surface filler is
off. Thereafter it is just a question
of going through the usual
polishing drill. Use transparent
white french polish.

TEN The common problems

F RENCH polishing is an art which can only be acquired with practice and experience. But if we can learn from other people's experience our mistakes will be fewer and less costly.

One of the ingredients which troubles beginners is raw linseed oil. After the wood has been stained a filler is used to fill the open pores of the grain. This is allowed to dry overnight before a little raw linseed is well rubbed in. The oil serves two purposes; it gives the filler a clear appearance and it brings up the figure of the grain. It must be rubbed in until the wood is dry otherwise there is a danger that at a later date it will sweat through the french polish.

During the bodying-up process a touch of raw linseed oil is applied to the face of the rubber to lubricate its progress and prevent it from dragging and consequently tearing up the soft shellac surface. Pour a little oil into a shallow container so that when lubrication is needed the tip of a finger may be dipped in the oil and wiped across the rubber. (Don't be like somebody I knew who stuck his finger into the neck of the oil bottle and couldn't get it out again).

If working with transparent white polish keep the linseed oil bottle well out of reach. Their appearances are not dissimilar and it has been known for a rubber to be charged with oil instead of polish. The resulting smeary mess is not to be recommended.

Be careful where you site your polish bottle when polishing. Have it to the end of the work rather than at the far side of it. In the latter position there is the risk that when re-charging the rubber you pick up the bottle and pour polish into the wadding right above the newly-polished surface. It only needs one drop to be spilled on to the soft lac below to ruin your previous efforts.

When using the rubber make sure that all the loose edges of the rag covering are gathered up into the palm of your hand. If pieces of trailing rag touch the newly-polished area they can leave a disfiguring mark. Similarly overall and shirt sleeves should be rolled up to prevent the cuffs from dragging on the work. Ladies should remove charm bracelets for the same reason.

The rubber should be pointed to enable it to be worked into awkward corners such as panelled doors and the fronts of cock-beaded drawers. For jobs such as turned legs or carvings it may not be possible to work the rubber into all the quirks, so the polish is applied with a bear hair mop. The mop has very soft bristles and if care is taken in applying the polish there will be no brush marks. The mop is obtainable in various sizes from polish suppliers.

With some jobs holding the

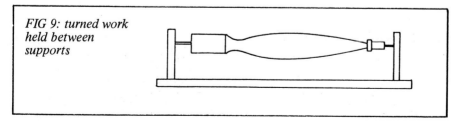

FIG 9: turned work held between supports

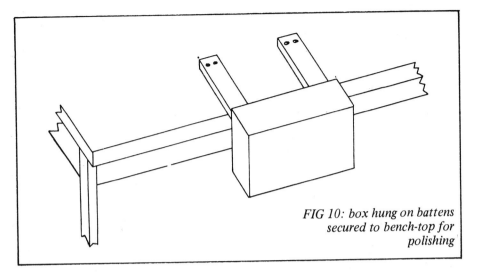

FIG 10: box hung on battens secured to bench-top for polishing

work can be a puzzle because the freshly-polished surfaces are too soft to be handled. Turned work such as candlesticks can be held between specially rigged centres (Fig 9) and polished with the mop. Trinket boxes can be difficult to polish all four sides at once but this is overcome by hanging the boxes on two battens secured to the bench (Fig 10). When one side has been polished the box is suspended by another side to allow another surface to be polished. Similar battens can be used to support drawers when polishing the fronts.

When both sides of a piece of work have to be polished (such as bureaux falls and grand piano lids)

some method has to be found to protect the newly-polished surface while the second surface is polished. This is where carpet sticks are useful. Battens of 2 x ¾in about 2ft long are covered with thick pile carpet. The join is tacked down the edge of the batten (Fig 11) and the whole covered in fine cotton to prevent fluff forming. Having polished one side of the work and allowed it to thoroughly harden the sticks are positioned to the bench and the polished face rested on them while the second side is completed.

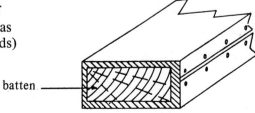

batten

FIG 11: batten covered in carpet and cotton

58

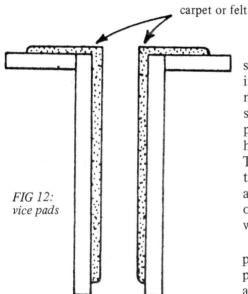

carpet or felt

FIG 12:
vice pads

Occasionally a finished piece such as a door has to be eased and if it were held in the vice in the normal way the polish would suffer. To prevent damage vice pads are required. These securely hold the work without marking. Two wooden vice jaws are nailed together and covered with carpet and cotton. The pads are slipped over the existing vice jaws and the work secured ready for easing.

When a panelled door is to be polished it helps if the panel is polished before the door is assembled. Holding a thin panel securely while being polished is achieved with the aid of a polishing board. This can be a sheet of plywood covered with two or three sheets of brown paper to protect the surfaces, with thin laths pinned round the edges to prevent movement. The laths, being thinner than the panel, stand below the surface being polished.

It would be possible to pin the panel to the board by driving pins through the edges of the panel which will later be covered by the mouldings of the framework. The snag is that the pins would have to be sunk below the surface to prevent the rubber catching on them and their subsequent withdrawal could split or damage the panel. The polishing board is held firmly on the bench either by G-clamps or dogs in the bench

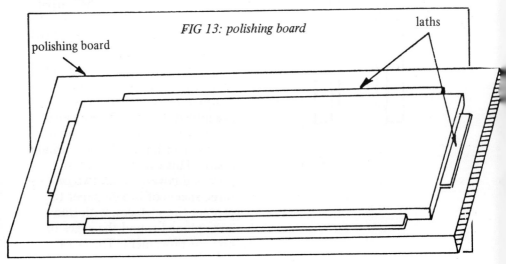

FIG 13: polishing board

polishing board

laths

top and tail vice.

In good-class work, and particularly pianos, the work is assembled and finished before the mouldings are screwed on from the back. The mouldings are numbered so that they are returned to their correct positions and are screwed from below to the polishing board. Beneath each moulding is placed a strip of cardboard slightly narrower than the moulding (Fig 14). By placing the mouldings parallel to each other the polishing rubber can easily be swept along them from one end to the other. If the contours of the mouldings have

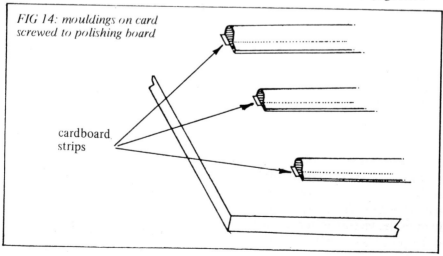

FIG 14: mouldings on card screwed to polishing board

cardboard strips

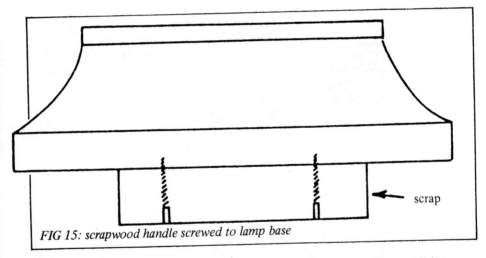

FIG 15: scrapwood handle screwed to lamp base

deep quirks in them it may be easier to apply the polish with a mop.

Small items such as lamp bases should have a small square of 1 in thick scrapwood screwed to the base (Fig 15). The scrapwood is held in the vice enabling all faces to be polished without handling them. As the lamp base will later be covered with green baize the screw holes, when filled, will never be seen.

63

The natural way to wax

By appointment to H M Queen Elizabeth II
Manufacturers of polishes and lacquers

HENRY FLACK (1860) LTD.
BECKENHAM KENT

For the initial finishing, care, or restoration of all types of wood furniture Henry Flack (1860) Ltd. has the quality products for every stage.

Firstly, there is BRIWAX for restoration work and for enriching new wood, ideal for Pine. It is available in Clear and six wood shades.

SHERADALE is a fine beeswax based polish to achieve a glow to the wood. It is available in Dark or Light tones.

There is also a full range of products: French Polishes, Varnishes, Strippers, Sealers, Stains, including Mr. Flack's Olde English Collection of Woodcare products and DIY kits.

Write or telephone for full details and brochure.

HENRY FLACK (1860) LTD
P.O. Box 78 BECKENHAM KENT
Telephone: 01 658 2299 Telex: 946804

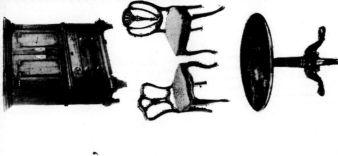
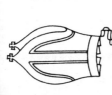

INDEX